Bruce
Byfield

Choosing Fonts

Designing with LibreOffice, Extract 2

Copyright

Editor & Publisher

Jean Hollis Weber, Friends of OpenDocument, Inc., 544 Carlyle Gardens, Beck Drive North, Condon, Queensland 4815, Australia. Please direct any comments or suggestions about this document to info@friendsofopendocument.com.

Reviewers

Jean Hollis Weber, Lee Schlesinger, Nicola Einarson, Terry Hancock, Charlie Kravetz, Michael Manning, Jean-Francois Nifenecker, Georges Rodier, Christina Teskey.

Special thanks also go to Marcel Gagné, Michael Meeks, and Carla Schroder for advanced reading.

Acknowledgments

Parts of this book's content were originally published, sometimes in different forms, by Linux Journal, Linux.com, Linux Pro Magazine, Open Content and Software, Wazi, and WorldLabel. My thanks for permission to re-use this material.

Publication date and software version

Published 10 August 2016. Based on LibreOffice Version 5.0.2.2 and later.

Photo credits

They depict the Sun Yat Sen Classical Garden in Vancouver, Canada. The gardens are based on the philosophy of feng shui, which, like typography, works deliberately to produce a natural, unnoticed effect. All photos are used with permission.

Table of Contents

Chapter 1

Chapter 2

For Trish, Always

1

Introduction

This book is an extract from a much larger book entitled *Designing with LibreOffice*. It is intended for those who only want information on choosing and using fonts with LibreOffice, the popular free-licensed office suite. It consists of Chapter 4 and Appendixes C & D in the larger book.

Although the first published extract, this book will eventually become the second of five excerpts from the complete book.

The excerpts will be:

Part 1: Styles and Templates

Part 2: Choosing Fonts

Part 3: Character and Paragraph Styles

Part 4: Page, Frame, and List Styles

Part 5: Slide Shows, Diagrams, and Spreadsheets

The emphasis in each book is design. In all of them, design is defined, not as formatting that calls attention to itself, like an HTML blink tag, but as formatting that is attractive and makes a document easy to read, edit, and maintain.

Together, the five smaller books will contain most, but not all the information from the larger book. Any changes are minimal, and made for continuity or changes in structure made necessary by the changes in format.

Tip

You can download the entire *Designing with LibreOffice* book or (when available) other excerpts from:

http://designingwithlibreoffice.com/download-buy/

Printed versions of the entire book or of excerpts are available for sale at the Friends of Open Document store at:

http://www.lulu.com/spotlight/opendocument

If you need information on features or selections that are not mentioned in this book, see the LibreOffice documentation page:

http://www.libreoffice.org/get-help/documentation/

Printed versions of the LibreOffice manuals are available for sale at the Friends of Open Document store at:

http://www.lulu.com/spotlight/opendocument

2

Fonts, color, and the magic number

The first step in designing a document is to choose its fonts. Your choices will determine not only the look of your document, but, in a well-designed document, other details of your design as well.

As you select fonts, constantly ask yourself: How appropriate is a font to your subject matter and requirements?

Often, answering this question is a matter of imagination. Typography may have worked out a general set of principles, but it remains an art more than a science. For instance, a modern geometric font may seem futuristic, and therefore more appropriate for science fiction.

At other times, the answer will be exact. For example, some fonts have characters that are so thin that they are invisible online or with a low resolution printer. Others may be so gray they are hard to read, or so black that their effect is overwhelming on the page.

However, whatever the conditions, the fonts you choose should never be more noticeable than the content. The choice of fonts is meant to enhance your content, not to make the layout the center of attention.

Finding fonts to use

Many users never venture beyond the fonts installed on their computers when they design documents. Nothing is wrong with that choice, but nothing is particularly right with it, either.

By using fonts that everyone has seen many times, you greatly increase the chance of creating an impression of blandness. Familiar fonts like Times Roman or Helvetica can work against you, because they encourage readers to pay less attention or unconsciously question the originality of your ideas.

Traditionally, more computer fonts are designed for sale like any other software. Design houses like Adobe sell hundreds, including official versions of famous fonts like Gill Sans or Didot.

For years, the only alternative to paying for fonts was to use public domain fonts, which were often low quality.

However, hundreds of free-licensed fonts are now available. Sometimes designed by more than one person and often for love of typography rather than for money, the best free-licensed fonts like Gentium easily rival commercial fonts.

Many Linux distributions include a few free-licensed fonts in their package repositories. For other places where you can find free-licensed fonts, see Appendix A, "Where to get free-licensed fonts," page 45.

Installing fonts for LibreOffice

Both LibreOffice and Apache OpenOffice support PostScript (.pfb), TrueType (.ttf), and OpenType (.otf) font file formats.

Other font formats exist, and may be supported by your operating system, but these formats may be limited in selection and quality.

If you have administration privileges, you can install additional fonts through your operating system. Otherwise, you can install fonts only for LibreOffice by placing their files in the /share/fonts folder in the system path listed at TOOLS > OPTIONS > PATH and restarting LibreOffice.

Choosing fonts in LibreOffice

The first step in design is to choose the fonts. They are chosen on the FONT tab of a paragraph or character style.

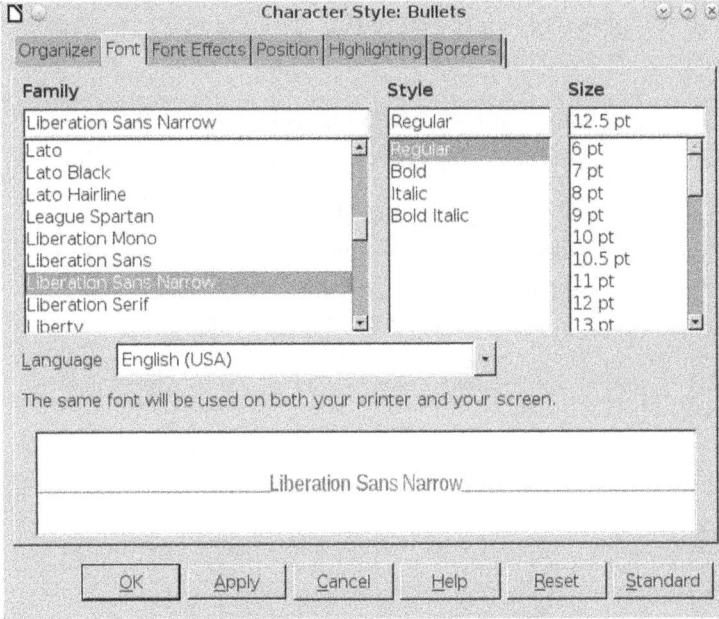

The FONT tab for character and paragraph styles.

On the FONT tab, each font has three basic characteristics: its family, its style or typeface (depending on the version and platform), and size. Fonts can be further modified by features on the FONT EFFECTS tab. See "Font Effects," page 23.

Font families

In LibreOffice, related fonts are called a family. The six main font families are:

- Serif: Fonts whose lines end with a foot or a hook.

  A sub-category of serifs is called slab serifs, and uses very large serifs, making them suitable for posters and online.

Serif **Slab**

Left: Serif font (Goudy Bookletter 1911). Right: Slab serif font (Chunk). The serifs on the slab serif are much thicker than on the ordinary serif.

- Sans serif: Literally, fonts whose lines lack the foot that characterizes serifs. Sans serif fonts often read well online.

  When the New Typography of the early twentieth century favored them as part of the general simplification of design, sans serif fonts gained a reputation for modernity that they still keep today. They are informally called Sans.

Sans Serif

Font: Raleway. A recent design, Raleway hints at a serif for the lower case "a," but its general tendency is sans serif.

- Monospace: Fonts in which every letter occupies exactly the same amount of horizontal space. By contrast, in most fonts, letters take up different amounts of space, with "i" taking up the least and "m" the most.

  Monospace fonts can be either serif or sans serif, but the sans serif monospace fonts usually look more contemporary.

Because of their association with typewriters, monospace fonts are unpopular today, except for specific uses such as writing code or movie scripts.

Monospaced

Font: Deja Vu Sans Mono. This font is included in most Linux distributions.

- Display: Unusual fonts, usually used only in short lines in a heading or on a pamphlet or ad.

DISPLAY

Font: Cinzel, a font based on Roman inscriptions.

- Script: Fonts that imitate cursive handwriting.

Script

Font: Pinyon-Script.

- Dingbat: Fonts in which pictures replace letters. Hundreds of dingbat fonts are available, from practical ones useful in charts and diagrams to fun ones with dinosaurs and medieval figures. Their advantage over clip art is that they are scalable; their disadvantage is that they only display in one color.

Font: Entypo.

Font styles

Different members of a font family are often called weights. This term is a reference to the thickness of the lines that make up the individual letters. In character and paragraph styles, LibreOffice refers to a weight as a font style or typeface.

The most common styles are:

- Roman: This is the font style most often used for body text. It may also called Regular, Book, or Medium, although these are not always exact synonyms in individual font families.

Sometimes a Narrow or Condensed version is available, in which the characters take up less width.

Roman

Font: ADF Romande.

- Italic: A cursive font, slanted to the right, used mainly for emphasis and book titles. In modern fonts, the Italic is sometimes replaced by an Oblique style, which is similar to the Roman, only inclined to the right.

Italic Oblique

Left Font: ADF Baskervald. Right Font: ADF Gillus.

- Bold: A version of the font with heavier lines on each character. Used for strong emphasis and headings, this weight sometimes replaces Italic online.

Variants may have names like Black, Semi-bold, Demi-bold, Extra, or Heavy, sometimes each with a different thickness of line. The thicker variations are usually intended for use at large font sizes in media like posters.

Bold Heavy

Left: Lato Bold. Right: Lato Ultra Black.

- Old Style Figures: Numbers which have no common baseline, originally designed in the Renaissance. Those who have studied typography often prefer them, even though, to a modern eye, they can look stuffy and be difficult to read. Their opposite, which most fonts have, are called lining figures, and are the numerals generally in use today.

1234567890

1234567890

Above: Old style figures. Font: Goudy Bookletter 1911.
Below: Lining figures. Font: Liberation Sans.

STOP

Caution

Avoid using old style figures in spreadsheets or in diagrams in which you want to align numbers. Their lack of a common baseline is distracting in long columns or tables of numbers, and they are difficult to position manually.

- Small Capitals (Small Caps): Specially designed upper case letters intended to make more than two capitals in a row more readable.

Tip

If you use old style figures for numbers, use small caps beside them. Normal caps look outlandishly large beside old style figures.

SMALL CAPS

REGULAR CAPS

Top: True small caps, created using the font's metrics. Bottom: Regular upper case letters. Small capitals are not only smaller than regular capitals, but also proportioned differently. Font: Fanwood.

Tip

In addition, some font families include styles such as Bold Italic, Thin, and Outline. A few fonts take a different approach, and divide fonts into Serif, Sans, and Monospace.

Real fonts vs. manufactured ones

Some fonts store metrics for different weights within the same file. Others have separate fonts for each weight, but if you change the weight while using the regular weight, you get manufactured versions of the different weights which have little resemblance to the real ones.

This problem is common with TrueType fonts, and when you change weights from the tool bar or a CHARACTER dialog window.

Italics

Italics

Top: Manufactured italics. Bottom: True italics. The angle on the manufactured italics makes them awkward and harder to read, and the letter shapes are frankly flights of fantasy. Font: Nobile.

bold

bold

Top: A manufactured bold style. Bottom: The bold style the designer intended. Notice the difference in spacing and letter shape. Font: Nobile.

SMALL CAPS

MANUFACTURED

REGULAR CAPS

Top: True small capitals. Middle: Manufactured small capitals for the same font. Bottom: Regular capitals. Font: Linux Libertine G.

Selecting fonts by font styles / typefaces

In theory, font styles should help you to choose fonts. However, in practice, font styles are inconsistent enough that the best they can give you is a rough indication of whether a font is suitable for your needs.

To start with, a font family traditionally contains four main styles: Regular, Italic, Bold, and Bold Italic. However, remember that just because two font styles have the same name does not mean you are under any obligation to use them together.

For instance, Nobile Italic is not actually an italic at all. Instead it is an oblique – the regular weight angled to the right. If you prefer an italic, you might go searching for something compatible with the regular weight.

Or perhaps an ampersand (&) figures in your design, but the font you want to use has a mundane design for ampersands. Just because the type designer thinks that font styles or individual characters fit together does not mean that you should accept their judgment.

& & & & &

Designers regularly borrow ampersands (and sometimes question marks) when they want an elegant touch. Fonts, from left to right: Cantarell, Quattrocento Roman , Goudy Bookletter 1911, Accanthis ADF Std., Lato.

Another point to consider is that you are rarely likely to need Bold Italic. Since the EMPHASIS character style uses Italic and STRONG EMPHASIS uses Bold, Bold Italic serves no regular purpose. It may be useful as a display or heading font, but often you can ignore a Bold Italic style if the other styles suit your needs.

Regular

Italics

Bold

Bold Italics

The four basic font styles in most font families. Up to a dozen other may also be included. Font: Nobile.

Another issue with font styles is that, through the years, various attempts have been made to standardize them. If you know CSS, you may recall how it categorizes font weights with three-digit numbers.

However, even in this summary, problems emerge. Italic and Oblique have no natural place, which is why you now see fonts designated as Italic or Oblique in their names. The same is true for Outline fonts, which show only the borders of characters but no fill.

Even more important, what looks like a well-regulated system at first glance is on closer look extremely arbitrary. The use of names is not standardized in 300-500, or 700-900, and, while in theory a font could have a weight of 350, what exactly would that mean, except in relation to other fonts in the same family? As an absolute measurement, it is almost meaningless.

100: Extra Light.

200: Light.

300: Book.

400: Regular, Roman.

500: Medium.

600: Semi-Bold/Demi-bold.

700: Bold.

800: Heavy, Extra, Black.

900: Ultra, Extra.

Font styles in CSS. Many fonts use the same classifications.

These cautions do not mean that font styles are not useful in deciding what fonts to use. But you do need to remember that all systems are approximate and relative to the font family. Always experiment thoroughly before selecting a font.

Font sizes

Traditionally, fonts are measured in points. In the digital age, this measurement has been standardized as one-seventy-second of an inch (or of 2.54 centimeters). Previously, a point was actually slightly less, but points remain defiantly non-metric and a sign of typographic expertise.

Tip

When you are setting up paragraph and character styles, go to TOOLS > OPTIONS > LIBREOFFICE WRITER > GENERAL > SETTINGS and change the MEASUREMENT UNIT to points.

Using points will make designing much easier because you have a consistent measurement. You can always change the MEASUREMENT UNIT back to centimeters or inches when you start to add content to a template.

The font size refers to the amount of space given to each character and the empty space around it. However, how each font uses the empty space can vary tremendously. Each font uses a different amount of empty space, which explains why the actual height of fonts of the same size is inconsistent. In fact, the actual height can vary considerably.

A A A

The font size for each of these capitals is the same, but the height of the letters varies. Fonts, from left to right, are League Spartan, Oxygen Sans, and Liberation Sans.

The standard size for body text is usually 10–14 points. Text for captions and notes sometimes goes as low as 8 points, while headings and titles are rarely more than 28 points.

Tip

LibreOffice's pre-defined heading paragraph styles express size as percentages of the Headings styles.

Since the size of all headings are usually determined at the same time and in relation to each other, using percentages is logical.

However, as shown later in this chapter, many design elements are based on the size of the standard fonts, which are most conveniently measured in points. For this reason, setting headings in points as well only makes sense.

You can force LibreOffice to display the size in points by placing the cursor in the SIZE field of the FONT tab, and entering the size followed by "pt."

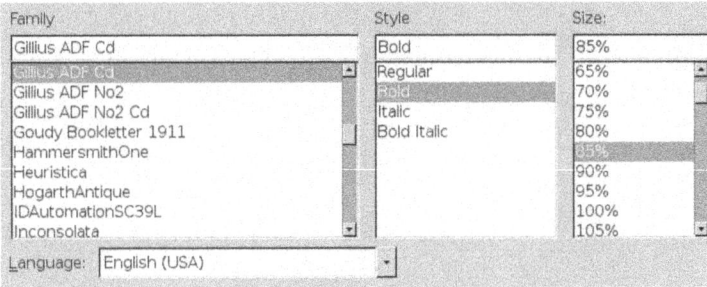

Family	Style	Size:
Gillius ADF Cd	Bold	85%
Gillius ADF Cd	Regular	65%
Gillius ADF No2	Bold	70%
Gillius ADF No2 Cd	Italic	75%
Goudy Bookletter 1911	Bold Italic	80%
HammersmithOne		85%
Heuristica		90%
HogarthAntique		95%
IDAutomationSC39L		100%
Inconsolata		105%

Language: English (USA)

Heading styles are measured by default in percentages because their size is often determined together.

Font Effects

The FONT EFFECTS tab contains a variety of features, with widely differing degrees of usefulness.

In most circumstances, the FONT COLOR and EFFECTS fields are the most useful. In particular, the EFFECTS field includes the option for SMALL CAPITALS, which are used to make two or more upper case letters in a row more readable.

By contrast, OVERLINING, STRIKETHROUGH, and UNDERLINING have limited use in most circumstances. All three are largely for the automatic use of LibreOffice when displaying changes in a collaborative document.

In all other cases, use the FONT EFFECTS tab cautiously. Effects such as SHADOW, BLINKING, or RELIEF are leftovers from when word processors were new and users over-indulged in all the effects they suddenly had. All these effects break the basic purpose of typography by calling attention to themselves while doing nothing to enhance the main text.

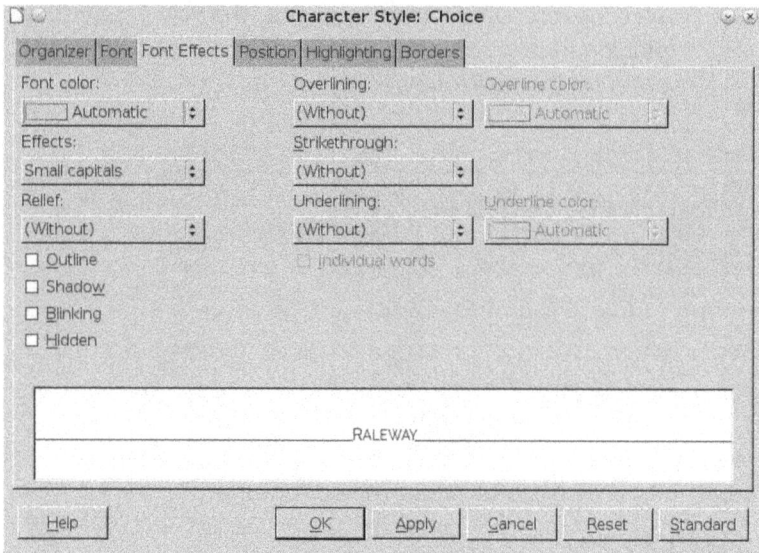

Character Style: Choice

Organizer | Font | Font Effects | Position | Highlighting | Borders

Font color:
☐ Automatic

Effects:
Small capitals

Relief:
(Without)

☐ Outline
☐ Shadow
☐ Blinking
☐ Hidden

Overlining:
(Without)

Strikethrough:
(Without)

Underlining:
(Without)

Overline color:
☐ Automatic

Underline color:
☐ Automatic

☐ Individual words

RALEWAY

Help | OK | Apply | Cancel | Reset | Standard

The FONT EFFECTS tab for character and paragraph styles. Many of the choices on this tab should be used sparingly, if at all.

Choosing basic fonts

The typographical convention is to limit each document to two font families: one for body text, and one for headings, headers, and footers. Any more tend to call attention to the design at the expense of the content.

However, this is not quite the limitation it sounds. The majority of fonts include a minimum of four font styles – Roman, Italic, Bold, and Bold Italic. Some have as many as nine, and a few have even more. Using so many font styles in the same document can look just as cluttered as too many different fonts, but nobody is likely to notice if you use several together.

A few fonts even come in pairs of a serif and a sans serif, and even a monospaced variation. These styles are more than enough for most needs. In fact, one font family is often all that is needed for effective design.

Judging fonts

To appreciate the differences between fonts, some typographical terms are useful:

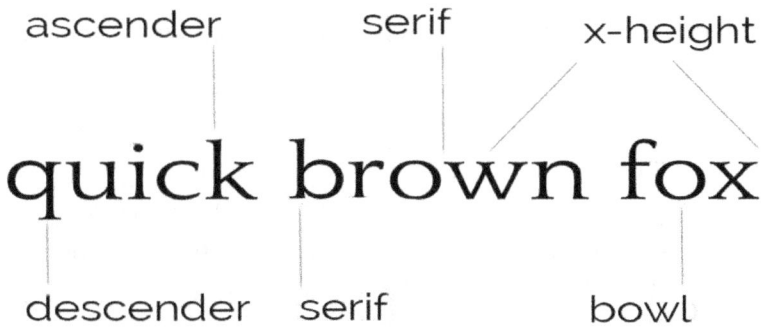

ascender   serif   x-height

quick brown fox

descender   serif   bowl

The basic terms to describe fonts physically.

- X-height: the height of a letter "x" and sixteen other letters.

- Ascenders and descenders: respectively, vertical strokes that rise above the baseline and descend below it.

- Bowls: The rounded parts of letters like "b," "d," and "o."

- Serifs: The small hooks at the bottom and top of ascenders and descenders found in some fonts.

If you study different font samples, you will see how these elements differ between fonts. This is the first step in learning how to appreciate fonts professionally. After all, if you have names for features, you can more easily observe them.

Choosing a body font

The first font you need is a body text. The main functional criterion for a body text font is that it must be easily readable by your audience in the conditions in which they are likely to see it.

For example, if you are designing a memo template for a low-resolution fax, you might prefer a larger, bold text style. Similarly, a brochure aimed at seniors might use a larger font size than usual out of respect for their failing eyesight. In other cases, you may be limited by a lower printer resolution or even a temporary shortage of toner to fonts with thick, consistent lines.

Tip

Often, a key feature for body text is the x-height. This is just what it sounds like: the height of the letter "x" and sixteen other lower case letters.

As a rule, the higher the x-height, the more readable a font is likely to be. However, if the ascenders and descenders are short, a high x-height might be less of an asset.

Choosing a heading font

The second font you probably need is for headings, headers, footers, and sub-headings – everything that guides readers through the document but is not actually content. It can belong to the same font family as the body text, but, if so, it should be a different font style, size, or color.

LibreOffice provides for up to ten heading levels, but this number is overkill. Any more than three or four levels of headings (including chapter titles) makes designing difficult and meaningless. Formatting ten heading levels so that each is distinct may just be possible, but neither the designer nor the reader is likely to be able to remember what all of them mean.

Other considerations for fonts

Choosing fonts begins with the impression you want to make. For instance, a commonly used font helps to put readers in an accepting mood, while a usual one might reinforce an impression of innovation.

At times, a font might need to fit the constraints of the page. A tall, narrow page, for example, might be matched with a similarly tall and narrow font. Or maybe a font has some association with the content – for instance, at least one edition of Arthur Conan Doyle's *The Hound of the Baskervilles* was printed in Baskerville font.

More general considerations can include:

- Where will the document be used? The North American convention is to use a serif font for body text, and a sans serif for headings. By contrast, in Europe, typographers are much less likely to abide by this convention. You can use a sans serif for body text in North America, but it may be perceived as avant-garde.

- Is the document for paper or online use? Even today, text on a screen is lower resolution than professional printing, and may be processed differently by the brain than words on a page. For online use, you want fonts to have regular shapes, with a minimum of tapering. Often, that means designing mainly with sans serifs and the occasional slab serif.

- Will recipients have the fonts installed on their computers to display the document properly? If you only want recipients to view the document, you can send a PDF file. Otherwise, you

might be better off sticking to the standard Times New
Roman, Arial or Helvetica, and Courier.

Tip

If you use Linux, and lack these fonts, look for the
Liberation fonts, which are designed to take up the
same space as the standard fonts.

- Is embedding fonts in the file a solution? LibreOffice has had
  font embedding since version 4.1.3.2. Embedding simplifies
  file-sharing, making it unnecessary for recipients to have the
  document's fonts.

  However, a file of 14 kilobytes balloons into one of 13.4
  megabytes when only two fonts are embedded. Add more, and
  a file with embedded fonts may become too large to send as an
  attachment, especially to an account that can only receive
  attachments of a certain size.

Tip

Currently, Apache OpenOffice does not support
embedding fonts.

- Do you prefer to use only free-licensed fonts? If so, you will
  be unable to use some of the best-known fonts, although you
  can sometimes find substitutes for them (see Appendix B,
  "Free-Licensed Equivalents for Standard Fonts," page 49).

  However, free-licensed fonts are often cost-free. They also
  mean that recipients only need an Internet connection to
  install the fonts they need.

Matching fonts

Modern typography usually uses separate fonts for body and heading text. Matching fonts is an art form rather than a science, but you can increase the odds of finding fonts that go together by selecting ones that:

- Share the same font family. Modern typographers sometimes design serif, sans serif, and monospaced fonts to be used together, which can be a great convenience.

STOP
Caution

An exception is the Liberation fonts, which are designed as replacements for Times Roman, Helvetica, and Courier, rather than for compatibility with each other.

- Are designed by the same typographer. A designer's preferences and habits may remain similar enough between fonts to give a common appearance.

- Have a large number of font styles, especially if you plan to use the same font for both body text and headings.

- Are inspired by the same historical era or are described in the same terms. Even if you are uncertain how a Humanist font (one based on Renaissance designs) differs from a Geometric font (one based on simple shapes), you can safely guess that the two are unlikely to go together. Of course, the more you know about the history of typography, the more you match fonts by their origins. See "Matching by historical categories," page 30.

- Occupy the same horizontal or vertical width. If nothing else, this criterion makes for a more symmetrical design.

However, no matter what criteria you use, the only way to be sure that fonts match is to experiment with them, both on-screen and by printing frequent hard copy samples.

Matching by historical categories

Fonts frequently defy easy categorizations. However, some general historical trends do exist, even though experts do not always agree on the features that identify trends, or where each font belongs.

Historical categories are not mentioned anywhere in LibreOffice, but you can sometimes match fonts by choosing ones from the same historical category.

Humanist serifs

Humanist serifs were originally fonts designed during the Renaissance, mostly by Italian designers – which is why a standard font is called Roman and a cursive font Italic. Humanist fonts are characterized by small x-heights, regular strokes, rounded bowls, small serifs, and a dark color. Some strokes may be angled, such as the crossbar on the lower case "e."

They are popular choices for body text today, although some designers think they look old fashioned.

The original Humanist fonts were also extremely dark, perhaps to make them more legible by candlelight. Modern imitations sometimes reduce the darkness to make them more acceptable to modern tastes.

Humanist serif

Font: Coelacanth, a free-licensed version of Bruce Roger's popular Centaur, which in turn was inspired by the work of Renaissance designer Nicholas Jenson.

Old Style

Sometimes an alternate name for Humanist serifs, "Old Style" is technically reserved for seventeenth-century designs or designs inspired by them.

Old Style fonts are characterized by wedge-shaped serifs, and their strokes show more variation in thickness than Humanist fonts. Like Humanist serifs, Old Style fonts are very popular for general purposes.

Old Style

Font: Linden Hill, a modern free-license rendering of Frederick Goudy's Deepdene.

Transitional

Also called Enlightenment, NeoClassical, and Modern, Transitional fonts first appeared during the Enlightenment. Their name refers to the fact that their serifs are small, anticipating the rise of sans serifs. Their strokes vary widely, their bowls are oval, and their serifs thin. Extreme versions, like the proprietary Didot, have strokes that are so thin that they almost disappear at small font sizes, or with a low-resolution printer.

Transitional

Font: Baskervald ADF, a free-licensed version of Hugo Baskerville's classic transitional font Baskerville.

Slab serifs

Slab serifs first appeared in the early 1800s. They are sometimes called Egyptian, because they were used in the publications of the research done in Egypt during Napoleon's invasion.

As their name implies, slab serifs have thick, broad serifs. Although often used for posters, some can be used for body text. Many are an exception to the conventional wisdom that serif fonts cannot be used online, and are often highly readable online or in slide shows.

Slab Serif

Font: Josefin Slab.

Sans serifs

Sans serif fonts are exactly what their French name implies: fonts without serifs. When they first appeared in the early nineteenth century, they were called "grotesque" and "gothic."

Modern sans serifs usually fall into one of two categories. Geometric fonts are marked by regular strokes and simple shapes, including circles for bowls. Geometric fonts were popular with Modernist schools for design.

Geometric

Font: Oxygen, the default for KDE's Plasma desktop in Linux.

By contrast, Humanist sans serif or Modern Humanist fonts are based on the clean lines of Roman inscriptions. Both the Arts and Crafts and Art Nouveau schools of design favored them, and they remain popular today.

Some Humanist sans serifs are versatile enough to be used for both headings and body text.

Humanist Sans

Font: Cantarell, the default font for the GNOME desktop in Linux.

Using dummy text to experiment

Dummy text is text unrelated to the document. It is used so you can focus on the result of formatting changes rather than the content.

The traditional dummy text in typography is the Lorem Ipsum, a passage so-called from its opening words. The Lorem Ipsum is fractured Latin, based on a passage from Cicero's essay, "The Extremes of Good and Evil," and can be downloaded from several sites.

Lorem ipsum dolor sit amet, consectetur adipisicing elit, sed do eiusmod tempor incididunt ut labore et dolore magna aliqua. Ut enim ad minim veniam, quis nostrud exercitation ullamco laboris nisi ut aliquip ex ea commodo consequat.

The start of the Lorem Ipsum, the popular dummy text passage.

The assumption behind the Lorem Ipsum is that, unless you can read Latin, you will not be distracted by the meaning of the words when you focused on formatting. For that matter, even if you read Latin, the passage is unlikely to distract you for very long, because you will see it so often that you will soon ignore the sense.

STOP Caution

Do not rely on the font preview in the FORMATTING tool bar or the sidebar. A single word is not enough to judge a font. At a minimum, you need several lines, while page design usually requires an entire page.

Study how the fonts you choose work together. They should not be jarringly different, but they should be sufficiently different for readers to tell them apart at a glance.

Look, too, for body text that fills a page or column without many hyphens. A sample riddled with hyphens is a sign that you will either have to change the font, or adjust its size or alignment.

As you work with a template, you will probably make changes the first few times you use it, including to the fonts.

However, you want a selection of fonts that will go together with a minimum of tweaking. If you need to fiddle too much with SCALE WIDTH or SPACING in a paragraph style, then finding another font is probably less effort for more aesthetic results.

Adjusting the page color

An important aspect of choosing fonts is the color of the body font. In this context, "color" does not refer to whether the text or the paper is black or green. Instead, color is the typographical term for how dark or light a passage or a page looks overall.

When you have found the line spacing that gives the color most pleasing to your eye, make a note of it. That line spacing is the magic number that can be the key to the rest of your design.

As you can see by opening professionally published books, you usually want the body text to be neither too black nor too washed out. Too black a color can be disturbing, while too washed out a color can be hard to read and looks like a publisher's error. Instead, you want a consistent dark gray.

The color of headings is usually darker than the body text, so it stands out when you are browsing. Otherwise, you can ignore the color of headings and concentrate on the body text.

Setting color through line spacing

The single most important influence on color is line-spacing. In LibreOffice, line spacing is set in the LINE SPACING field on the INDENTS & SPACING tab for paragraphs.

Line spacing is defined as the measurement from one baseline (the imaginary line that the bottom of a letter like "n" or "m" sits on) to the next one.

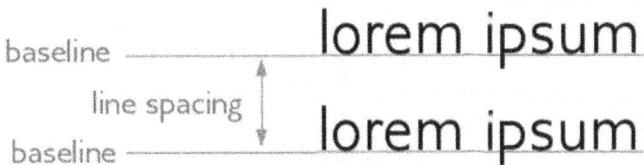

baseline ———————— **lorem ipsum**

   line spacing

baseline ———————— **lorem ipsum**

Line spacing is the distance between two baselines.

In LibreOffice Writer, line spacing appears to be set by the font size. The exact measurement is displayed when you set the LINE SPACING field to FIXED.

For convenience, typographers notate line spacing after the font size, so that a paragraph set in 12/14 has a 12 point font size and 14 points of line spacing.

When a paragraph's font size and line space are identical – for instance, 12/12 – then the paragraph is said to be "set solid." However, you rarely see a paragraph set solid except for short lines of text in brochures or ads, because the lines look crowded except with a few fonts with small letter sizes with plenty of white space around them.

lorem ipsum dolor sit amet, consectetur adipiscing elit. Int dapibus diam. Sed nisi. Nulla quis sem at nibh elementum nec tellus sed augue semper porta. Mauris massa. Vestibu sociosqu ad litora torquent per conubia nostra, per incept dignissim lacinia nunc. Curabitur tortor. Pellentesque nibh. mattis. Sed convallis tristique sem. Proin ut ligula vel nunc suscipit quis, luctus non, massa. Fusce ac turpis quis ligula

A font set solid (in this case, 12/12). With so little line spacing, the text is cramped and hard to read. Font: Universalis ADF STD.

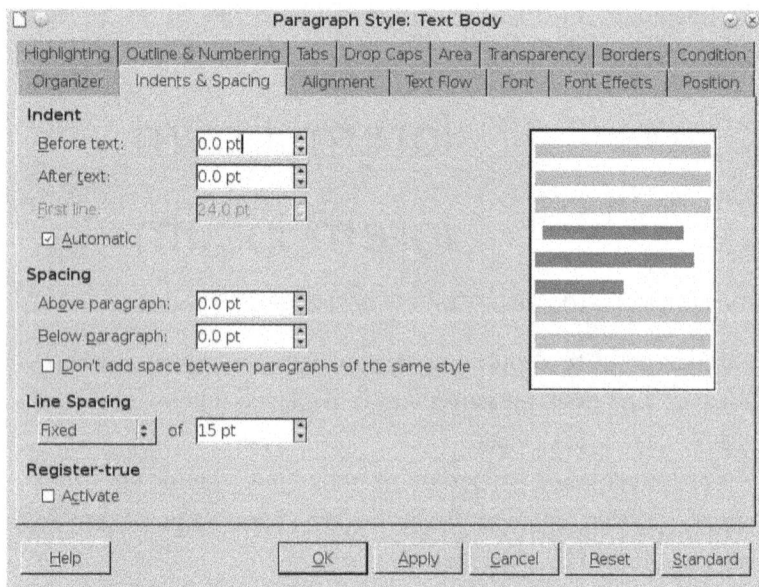

The INDENTS & SPACING tab. The color is adjusted mainly by setting the LINE SPACING field to a fixed distance.

LibreOffice sets a default line spacing based on the font size. For a 12 point font, that average is just over 14 points. However, because each font uses the space for characters differently, the default line spacing is not always ideal.

Tip

LibreOffice used to allow you to set line spacing to one-tenth of a point (1/720th of an inch). However, starting with the 4.2 release, you can only set line spacing to the nearest point. While you might not think such a small measurement would make a difference, it often can. By contrast, Apache OpenOffice still allows settings of 1/10 points.

When you have found the line spacing that gives the best color, make a note of it. That magic number can be the key to much of the rest of your design.

Caution

Typography calls line-spacing "leading," because of the pieces of metal that were once inserted between lines of text on a printing press.

However, LibreOffice uses "fixed" to refer to leading, and "leading" to refer to space in addition to the font size.

Contexts for changing color

Developing an eye for line spacing takes practice. Acceptable color may also depend to a degree on culture, era, and the principles of different design schools. However, certain contexts are more likely to need adjustments in line spacing than others. Experiment until you get acceptable results.

Increase spacing for:	Decrease spacing for:
• Fonts whose characters are narrow or have smaller spaces between them. (Adjusting SCALE WIDTH and SPACING on the POSITION tab may help as well.)	• Fonts whose characters are broad and have relatively large spaces between them.
• A line of text greater than about 80 characters.	• A line of text less than 45 characters.
• Font sizes of less than 10 points, or more than 14.	• Fonts of 10–14 points.
• Roman fonts that are too black.	• Roman fonts that are light gray.
• Most sans-serif fonts.	• Some serif fonts.
• Any italic or oblique font.	

Deciding whether to increase or decrease font spacing.

Applying the magic number

Beginning typographers often wonder how to proportion documents. Over the years, countless theories have evolved, many of them uncomfortably elaborate. But the easiest is what I call – for want of a better name – the magic number.

The magic number is the line spacing that gives the preferred color with the chosen Body Text font. Its application is simple: whenever possible, any measurement in a document will be a multiple of the selected line spacing.

Not every design element can use the magic number, but most of the important ones can:

- Text indents.
- First line indent.
- Space above paragraph.
- Space below paragraph.
- Space between numbers/bullet and list items.
- The space above or below a graphic or any other inserted object.
- Tabs.
- Page margins.
- Header/footer height.
- Space between a header and footer and main text.
- The combination of heading font size, the space above/below.

Some design elements to be adjusted using multiples of the magic number.

At times, you might use half the line spacing instead of a whole multiple. In theory, you could use quarter-line spacing, or an even smaller fraction, but that is harder to track.

Just as importantly, half line-spacing quickly puts spacing back to the magic number itself. As you design, you may want to keep a calculator handy, or else jot down a palette – a list of the multiples or half-multiples that you will be using.

5	10	15	20	25	30	35	40	45	50	55	60	70
5.5	11	16.5	22	27.5	33	39.5	44	50.5	55	61.5	66	72.5
6	12	18	24	30	36	42	48	54	60	66	72	78
6.5	13	19.5	26	32.5	39	45.5	52	58.5	65	71.5	78	84.5
7	14	21	28	35	42	49	56	63	70	77	84	91
7.5	15	22.5	30	37.5	45	52.5	60	67.5	75	82.5	90	97.5

A line-spacing palette for typical body text. All measurements are in points and can be used for setting other sizes and spacing. Font: Cinzel.

Using the magic number is painstaking – but it is precise and unambiguous. You should have no trouble detecting a document designed with the magic number, because of its unified appearance.

Example: Solving the magic numbers

Page color can be affected by many variables, including the designer's eye, the paper, and the toner left in the printer. Sometimes, it can be subjective, particularly if your eyesight is imperfect. However, at the very least, you should be able to make the page color regular, even if the tone could be improved.

In fact, the variables are so numerous that, each time you use a font, you need to ask yourself if the circumstances are different enough that you need to re-test the color.

Do not assume that because a color worked once, it will work equally well under other circumstances. Choosing the page color is always highly contextual, and small changes in formatting can sometimes have large effects.

Always experiment systematically. Increase the font size and line-spacing a bit at a time, and work with different combinations systematically. Making large changes will only waste time by forcing you to backtrack.

If you are lucky, LibreOffice's default settings of 12/14 (font size = 12 points, line-spacing = 14 points) may require no tweaking. In my experience, 20–35% of fonts need no adjustments.

For example, here is Josefin Slab without modifications:

Lorem ipsum dolor sit amet, consectetur
diam. Sed nisi. Nulla quis sem at nibh el
sed augue semper porta. Mauris massa.
torquent per conubia nostra, per inceptos
Curabitur tortor. Pellentesque nibh. Aene
tristique

Font: Josefin Slab, 12/14.

The font size might be increased, but on the whole Josefin Slab's default color is acceptable as is. That is just as well, because a couple of extra points between each line can add dozens of pages to a book and increase its production cost.

However, other fonts require testing, changing the font size and line-spacing one at a time, and trying out different combinations.

For example, at the default 12/14, E. B. Garamond's color is acceptable, but the height of the upper cases letters is unusually high, and makes the lines a little pinched. Changing the line spacing to 12/16 improves the layout:

Lorem ipsum dolor sit amet, consectetur ad
nisi. Nulla quis sem at nibh elementum imp
porta. Mauris massa. Vestibulum lacinia arc

Lorem ipsum dolor sit amet, consectetur adi
nisi. Nulla quis sem at nibh elementum imp
porta. Mauris massa. Vestibulum lacinia arc

Font: Above, E.B. Garamond, 12/14. Below: E.B. Garamond, 12/16.

Humanist fonts designed in the Renaissance were often designed to be very black by modern standards. Since that is the way they are meant to be seen, trying to lighten them would fail to do them justice.

Not every modern Humanist Serif is as dark as its inspirations, but many are. An example is Colecanth:

Lorem ipsum dolor sit amet, conse cursus ante dapibus diam. Sed nisi. ipsum. Praesent mauris. Fusce nec arcu eget nulla. Class aptent taciti himenaeos. Curabitur sodales ligul Pellentesque nibh. Aenean quam. I tristique

Font: Humanist (Coelacanth), 12/14.

Should you encounter a modern font that remains very dark despite all adjustments, that is probably a sign that it Is designed for headings or as a display font, and should not be used for body text.

If you really want to use a font with a dark color, try changing the width of characters from POSITION > SCALING, or the spacing between fonts from POSITION > SPACING.

For example, after wrestling Heuristica to a setting of 12/16, I found it still too dark, so I set the Spacing to add .8 of a point more between characters.

Even then, the font was darker than ideal, but much more increased space between letters would have destroyed the look of the font completely.

Under the circumstances, this final modification was the best I could manage, and is still darker than ideal:

Lorem ipsum dolor sit amet, consectetur adipiscing elit. Integer nec odio. Praesent libero. Sed cursus ante dapibus diam. Sed nisi. Nulla quis sem at nibh elementum imperdiet. Duis sagittis ipsum. Praesent mauris. Fusce nec tellus sed augue semper

Lorem ipsum dolor sit amet, consectetur adipiscing elit. Integer nec odio. Praesent libero. Sed cursus ante dapibus diam. Sed nisi. Nulla quis sem at nibh elementum imperdiet. Duis sagittis ipsum. Praesent mauris. Fusce nec tellus sed augue semper

Font: Above, Heuristica 12/14. Below, Heuristica 12/16, with .8pts of extra spacing between characters.

At other times, if all else fails, try a different font style. Raleway Thin, to take one example, is too pale for body text. (Perhaps it is meant to add a shadow?) Changing the font size or the space between characters worked slightly, but not enough.

In the end, I concluded that I was using Raleway Thin for a purpose that it was simply not intended for, and switched to Raleway's Regular weight instead.

Lorem ipsum dolor sit amet, consec cursus ante dapibus diam. Sed nisi. ipsum. Praesent mauris. Fusce nec

Lorem ipsum dolor sit amet, conse cursus ante dapibus diam. Sed nisi ipsum. Praesent mauris. Fusce nec

Font: Above, Raleway Thin 12/14. Below: Raleway Regular, 12./14.

The lesson in these examples? LibreOffice's defaults may not be what you need, so experiment as widely as possible as you search for the best possible page color. Too much depends on it for you settle for anything less.

An unexpected journey

This excerpt started with selecting fonts, but it ends well into character and paragraph styles. If you want to learn more about character and paragraph styles, look for *Designing with LibreOffice, Extract 3: Character and Paragraph Styles.*

A

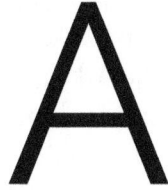

Where to get free-licensed fonts

Like free or open source software, free-licensed fonts are ones that you can use, share, and edit as you please. Most are also available at no cost.

Free-licensed fonts barely existed before 2000. By contrast, hundreds are available today, although their numbers are still small compared to the thousands of proprietary fonts available from font foundries such as Adobe.

Many are clones or near-variations of classic fonts, but some are original fonts that are outstanding by any definition. Both clones and originals help you work without using proprietary fonts.

Free-licensed fonts are available under the SIL Open Font License (OFL) or the GNU General Public License (GPL) with font exception. Some are also in the public domain. Other licenses exist, but not all have been evaluated by the Free Software Foundation or the Open Source Initiative, and should be used cautiously.

If you use Linux, some of these fonts can be installed as packages from your distribution's repositories. Many of the others can be downloaded online, regardless of operating system.

Arkandis Digital Foundry
(http://arkandis.tuxfamily.org/adffonts.html)
The Arkandis fonts are meant to provide free-licensed versions of fonts for Linux. The selection includes Baskervald (Baskerville), Gillius (Gill Sans), and Universalis (Univers), as well as original fonts such as Mint Spirit, which was originally designed as the unofficial font for the Linux Mint distribution.

Barry Schwartz
(http://crudfactory.com/font/index)
Barry Schwartz is one of the outstanding designers of free-licensed body text fonts. His work includes three fonts based on the designs of Frederick Goudy, as well as Fanwood, an understated font which closely resembles Eric Gill's Joanna. You can get also get some of his fonts from The League of Movable Type (see below).

Cantarell
(https://git.gnome.org/browse/cantarell-fonts/)
The official font for GNOME 3. Originally criticized for some of its letter forms, Cantarell has evolved into a modern humanist font that can be used for body text and headings alike.

Dover Books
(http://www.doverbooks.co.uk/Fonts,_Lettering.html)
Dover Books publishes about 30 books with CDs of fonts and dingbats from Victorian times and earlier. They are marked as "permission free," which presumably means public domain.

Google Fonts
(https://www.google.com/fonts/)
Featuring over 630 font families, Google Fonts is intended

mainly for online use. However, you can also download fonts for print use. Updates are regular, so check regularly for new releases of updates of existing fonts.

The League of Moveable Type
(https://www.theleagueofmoveabletype.com/)

Describing itself as "the first ever open-source type foundry," The League of Moveable Type offers a small but select library of original font designs. If you find yourself getting lost in the sheer number of free fonts, anything from The League can be counted on to be of high quality, and its fonts usually includes small capitals and old style figures.

Liberation Fonts
(https://fedorahosted.org/liberation-fonts/)

Liberation fonts are designed to be the metrical equivalent of standard proprietary fonts. In other words, they occupy the same vertical and horizontal space, although they may otherwise be designed differently. Liberation Sans is meant to substitute for Arial and Helvetica, Liberation Serif for Times New Roman, and Liberation Mono for Courier.

Open Font Library
(http://openfontlibrary.org/)

With over 400 font families, the Open Font Library is second only to Google Fonts in its selection. Its front page includes a list of the most recently uploaded fonts.

Oxygen
(http://www.fontspace.com/new-typography/oxygen)

Created for the KDE desktop environment on Linux, Oxygen is a modern geometric font, made of simple shapes, but highly readable and pleasing to the eye.

Raph Levien
(http://levien.com/type/myfonts/)

A Google employee, Levien also develops fonts in his spare time. Although not all the fonts displayed on this page are complete, their consistently high quality makes them worth considering. Most must be exported via the free-licensed font editor Fontforge to a usable format .

SIL International
(http://www01.sil.org/computing/catalog/show_software_catalog.asp?by=cat&name=Font)

SIL International is a missionary organization that specializes in fonts for minority languages. It also developed the Graphite system for the automatic use of ligatures, small caps, old style figures, and other advanced typographical features. The SIL Font License is the most widely used license for free fonts, and responsible for much of the spread of free fonts.

Ubuntu
(http://font.ubuntu.com/)

Designed for the Ubuntu Linux distribution, this is a modern humanist font. It is versatile, although its use in branding may mean that a document that uses it will be automatically be identified with Ubuntu.

B

Free-Licensed Equivalents for Standard Fonts

Like Linux desktops, free-licensed fonts started as imitations of proprietary equivalents. Today, original free fonts are becoming increasingly common, but the demand for free equivalents of proprietary fonts remains. This demand is unlikely to disappear because, although most professional designers think in terms of proprietary fonts, clients are often unwilling to pay for them. Moreover, free software advocates prefer free fonts to go along with their free applications.

Exact equivalents are rare because of fear of copyright restrictions. A match as high as 75% is rare. Some equivalents, such as the Liberation fonts, are only metrical – that is, they take up the same space as their proprietary equivalents, but the letters themselves are different. In other cases, the free fonts are inspired by their proprietary counterparts, but the designer never intended exact copies, and the most you can expect is a general resemblance. A few proprietary fonts, such as Optima, have no free equivalent at all, so far as I can see. For this reason, the listings in the table below are mostly the closest equivalents, and rarely exact replicas.

All of these fonts can be found from the sources listed in Appendix A.

Proprietary	Free Licensed
Alternate Gothic #1	League Gothic
Arial	Liberation Sans,* Pt Sans, Open Sans Condensed, Lato, Arimo*
Arial Narrow	Liberation Sans Narrow*
Avenir	Mint Spirit No2, Nunito
Baskerville	Baskervald ADF Standard, Libre Baskerville
Bembo	EB Garamond
Bodoni	Accanthis-Std, Oranienbaum, GFS Bodoni, Libre Bodoni
Cambria	Caladea*
Calibri	Carlito*
Caslon	Libre Caslon
Centaur	Coelacanth
Century Gothic	Muli
Comic Sans	Comic Relief
Courier	Liberation Mono,* Cousine*
Courier 10 Pitch	Courier Code
Courier New	Cousine
Didot	GFS Didot
Eurostile	Jura
Frutiger	Istok Normal 400
Futura	Mint Spirit No2, Nunito
Futura Light	Futura Renner Light

Garamond**	Crimson Text, EB Garamond
Georgia	Nimbus Roman No. 9
Gill Sans	Cabin, Gillius ADF, Hammersmith
Goudy Old Style**	Goudy Bookletter 1911, Linden Hill, Sort Mills
Helvetica	Liberation Sans,* Pt Sans, Open Sans Condensed, Lato
Helvetica Narrow	Liberation Sans Narrow*
Joanna	Fanwood
Letter Gothic	Josefin Sans, Josefin Slab
Myriad	Junction, Pt. Sans
News Gothic	News Cycle
Stone Sans	Nunito
Stone Serif	Lustria
Tahoma	Lucida Sans, Nimbus Sans
Times New Roman	Liberation Serif,* Linux Libertine, Tinos*
Trajan	Cinzel
Univers	Universalist-std
Verdana	DejaVu Sans

* Metrical equivalents.

** "Garamond" and "Goudy" are generic names for fonts inspired by particular designers, so the actual typefaces with these names can be very different from one another.

Index